Pebble® Plus

An Astronaut's LIFE

# Life in SPACE

by Martha E. H. Rustad

CAPSTONE PRESS
a capstone imprint

Pebble Plus is published by Capstone Press,
1710 Roe Crest Drive, North Mankato, Minnesota 56003
www.mycapstone.com

Library of Congress Cataloging-in-Publication data is available on the Library of Congress website.
ISBN 978-1-5157-9817-0 (library binding)
ISBN 978-1-5157-9821-7 (paperback)
ISBN 978-1-5157-9825-5 (eBook PDF)

**Editorial Credits**
Abby Colich, editor; Kyle Grenz, designer; Tracy Cummins, media researcher;
Kathy McColley, production specialist

**Photo Credits**
NASA Image and Video Library: Cover, 5, 7, 9, 11, 13, 15, 17, 19, 21; Shutterstock: Aphelleon,
Design Element, d1sk, Back Cover, Design Element, Zakharchuk, Design Element

## Note to Parents and Teachers

The An Astronaut's Life set supports science standards related to space. This book describes and
illustrates daily life in space. The images support early readers in understanding the text. The
repetition of words and phrases helps early readers learn new words. This book also introduces
early readers to subject-specific vocabulary words, which are defined in the Glossary section. Early
readers may need assistance to read some words and to use the Table of Contents, Glossary, Read
More, Internet Sites, Critical Thinking Questions, and Index sections of the book.

Printed and bound in the USA.
010768S18

# Table of Contents

# Life in Space

What if you put down this book,

and it floated up? That is what happens

in space. There is less gravity.

Everything floats. It makes

life in space different from Earth.

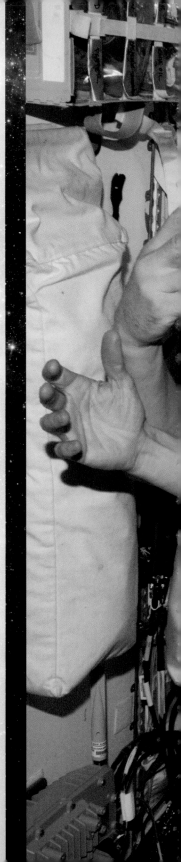

# Self Care in Space

Every morning astronauts wake up.

It's time to eat! There is no fridge in space.

Astronauts eat freeze-dried meals.

They add water to the food.

Then they heat it in an oven.

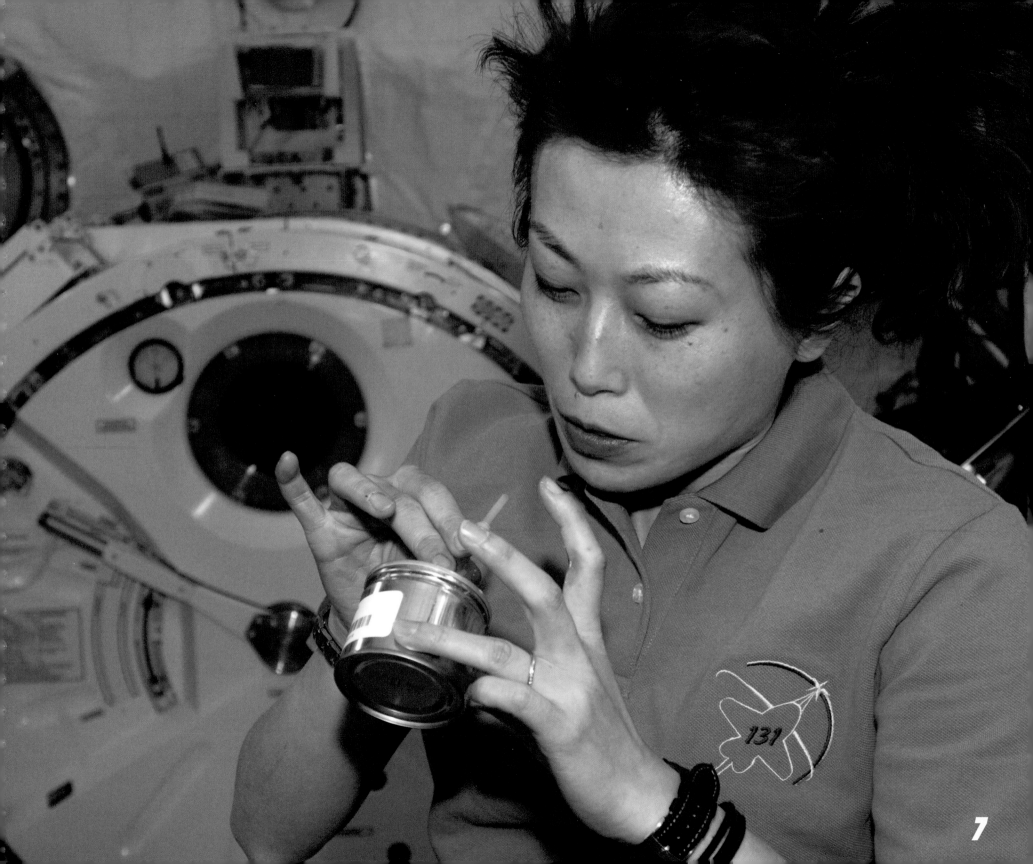

With less gravity, muscles become weak.

Astronauts must exercise every day.

They run on treadmills. They lift weights.

Sweat doesn't drip. They wipe it away

with a towel.

Toilets on Earth flush using water.

A space toilet uses moving air.

It's like a vacuum. The toilet cleans

the pee. Poop goes into a tube.

Then it gets burned with other trash.

Astronauts cannot take showers or baths.

The water would float everywhere!

They use a damp towel

to stay clean. No-rinse shampoo

cleans their hair.

In space astronauts don't do laundry.

There is no washing machine.

Instead, they change clothes
every few days.

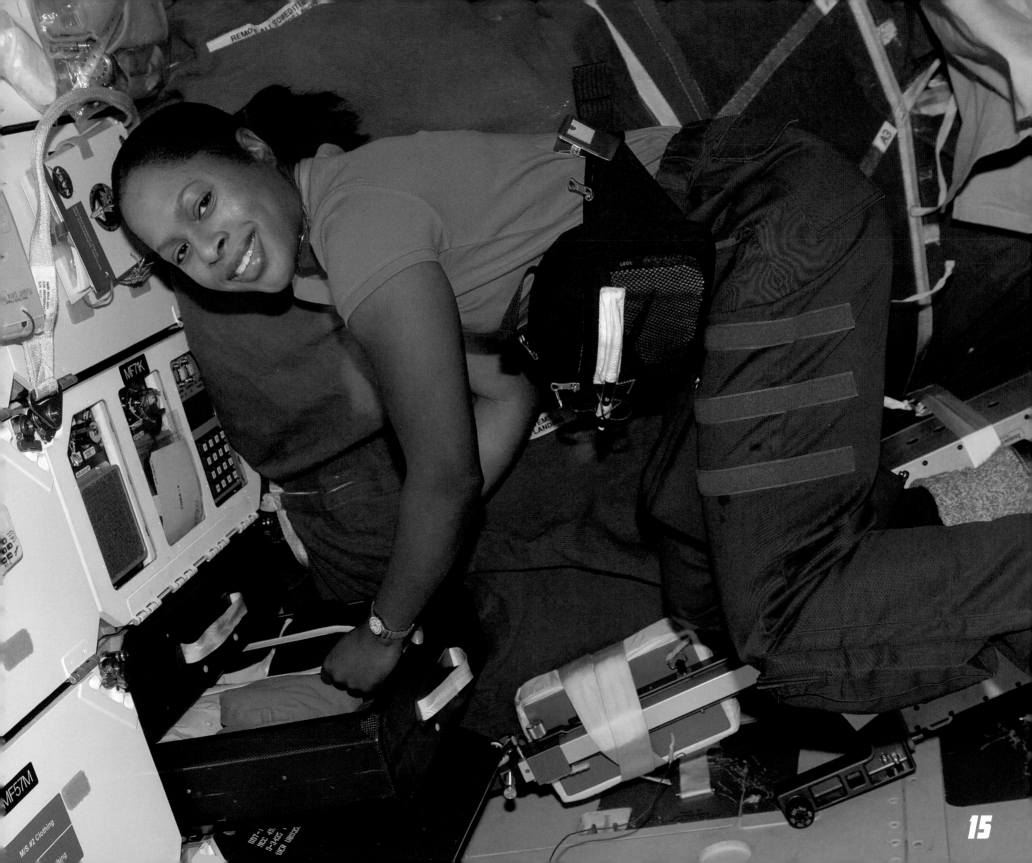

# Space Work and Play

Astronauts work hard.
They do experiments. They fix broken
space station parts. But they have
time off too. They read books
and watch movies.

Astronauts go to space for a long time.

They are far from home.

They miss their families and friends.

E-mails and video calls

help them stay in touch.

At the end of the day, astronauts are tired.

They don't lie down. They would just float up!

Each person has a tiny cabin.

A sleeping bag sticks to the wall.

Straps hold astronauts in place. Good night!

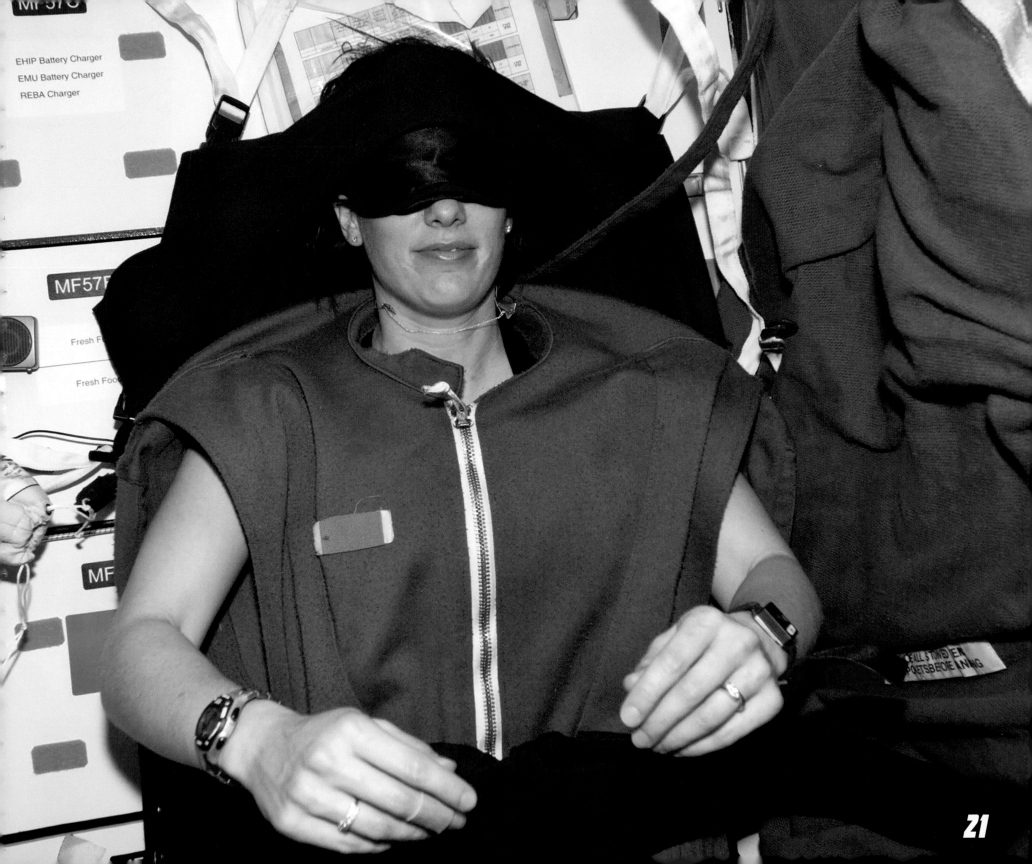

# GLOSSARY

**cabin** (KA-buhn)—a section in a spacecraft where crew members rest and relax

**e-mail** (EE-mayl)—an electronic message that is sent between computers

**experiment** (ik-SPEER-uh-muhnt)—a test to find out how something works

**freeze-dried** (FREEZ-DRIDE)—food that is preserved by removing water from it

**gravity** (GRAV-uh-tee)—a force that pulls objects with mass together; gravity pulls objects down toward the center of Earth

**space station** (SPAYSS STAY-shuhn)—a spacecraft that circles Earth in which astronauts can live for long periods of time

**treadmill** (TRED-mil)—a machine a person walks or runs on for exercise

# READ MORE

Clay, Kathryn. *Living in Space.* Little Astronauts. North Mankato, Minn.: Capstone, 2017.

Jones, Tom. *Ask the Astronaut: A Galaxy of Astonishing Answers to Your Questions on Spaceflight.* Washington, D.C.: Smithsonian Books, 2016.

West, David. *Lots of Things You Want to Know about Astronauts: . . . And Some You Don't!* Mankato, Minn.: Smart Apple Media, 2016.

# INTERNET SITES

Use FactHound to find Internet sites related to this book.

Visit *www.facthound.com*

Just type in 9781515798170 and go!

Super-cool stuff!

Check out projects, games and lots more at
**www.capstonekids.com**

# CRITICAL THINKING QUESTIONS

1. Name two ways astronauts exercise in space.

2. Look at the photo on page 13 and reread the text on the opposite page. What is the astronaut doing in this photo?

3. Reread the text on page 10. What would happen if you tried to use a toilet from Earth in space?

# INDEX